Adam Deceived

Freemasonry:
The World's Greatest Deception

Jim Shouse

authorHOUSE®

AuthorHouse™
1663 Liberty Drive, Suite 200
Bloomington, IN 47403
www.authorhouse.com
Phone: 1-800-839-8640

First published by AuthorHouse 3/24/2009

ISBN: 978-1-4389-3576-8 (sc)

Printed in the United States of America
Bloomington, Indiana

This book is printed on acid-free paper.

TABLE OF CONTENTS

Introduction

In the book of Genesis, we find the account of Adam and Eve in the Garden of Eden, and here we find that they were told not to eat the fruit of the tree that stood in the midst of the garden. This was the tree of the knowledge of good and evil. God told them that when they ate it, in that day, they would surely die. Gen. 2: 16,17. The serpent or (Satan), approached Eve in the garden and said, "Has GOD indeed said, 'You shall not eat of every tree of the garden? Eve replied, "We may eat the fruit of all the trees of the garden; but of the fruit of the tree which is in the midst of the garden, GOD has said, 'You shall not eat it nor shall you touch it, lest you die." And Satan said to the woman, "You will not surely die! For GOD knows that in the day you eat it, your eyes will be opened, and you will be like GOD, knowing good and evil". Gen. 3: 1-5.

Eve looked at the fruit and decided that it was pleasing to the eye and appeared good to eat, and would make one wise. So she took of the fruit and ate it. She was deceived by Satan, in the form of the serpent. She then gave to Adam, and he ate of the fruit. Any Bible scholar will tell you that Eve was <u>deceived</u> by Satan. Adam was <u>not</u> deceived. He knew what he was doing. He knew they were not supposed to eat of it. Consequently, GOD cast them from the Garden of Eden; drove them from it, lest they eat of the tree of Life and live-forever. HE told Adam that by the sweat of his brow, he would earn bread, and the ground would bring forth briars and thistles to plague him, and to resist his efforts to grow food. GOD told Eve that her pain would be greatly increased in childbearing. From this account, we see that the woman was deceived; the man was not. In 1 Timothy 2: 13,14 the writer, PAUL, tells us that Adam was not deceived, but Eve was. Man was first created, then the woman.

The intent of this book is to show that MAN can also be deceived. I know firsthand, because I was deceived at one time. It appears that man is sometimes more susceptible to deception than a woman, especially, if the deception is perpetrated by other men.

Chapter One
A Dream Takes Shape

At the age of four years, my eyes caught sight of a wonderful invention that crossed the sky above me. A biplane, most probably, an old Stearman, fascinated me as it flew across the sky at the unheard of speed of fifty or so miles per hour. That's for me, I decided then and there! From that point on, this wonderful invention that allowed a man to soar as a bird held my interest and curiosity. It was a great treat to see an automobile, let alone an airplane, in the hills of Northeastern, Mississippi, in the 1930's. So this sight motivated me to read and learn all that I could as I grew up and progressed through the grades of High School and Community College. Somewhere, I read that in flying, one needed mathematics and physics. Therefore, to this end, I applied myself diligently. In my Associate of Arts Degree, my major was Pre-Engineering with heavy emphasis on Math and Physics. Since my graduation from Community College came during the Korean War, I decided to test for the Aviation Cadet Program and enter the United States Air Force. I had no desire to enter the U.S. Army through the draft program. After a week of training, I was advised that I had passed for Navigation or Observer Training, but not for pilot training! This did not please me, but this training at least involved flying, and appealed to me more than Army Training.

I enlisted in the United States Air Force and entered Aviation Cadet Training. This training entailed thirteen months of military, academic, and flying training, upon which a commission as a Second Lieutenant was earned. Afterward, additional training was given for Navigation and other Observer positions of non-pilot jobs. After earning my wings as a Navigator, I then navigated a KC-97 aerial tanker for about four years, performing rendezvous and refueling, in-flight, bomber and fighter aircraft. Then, one day, while checking my records at Wing Headquarters, I found my initial scores for Pilot Training. Lo and Behold, I had passed for Pilot Training in the initial tests! The Air Force needed Navigators and Observers at that time very badly. I retook the exams and reapplied for pilot school. This training was much easier for me than Navigation, and I graduated with distinction, which earned me a Regular Commission later in my career. Now, I was triple rated as Pilot, Navigator, and Observer, and looked forward to my continuing career as an Air Force Officer.

I completed a one-year tour of duty in Southeast Asia during the Vietnam War, and returned to the USAF Inspector General's Office at Norton AFB, California. This duty involved flying Inspection Teams worldwide in C-118 type aircraft. This was a DC-6B, four-engine propeller driven aircraft configured for long passenger trips. While at this base and in this type of service, my career took a serious downward trend.

While serving as a commissioned officer in any branch of military service, one individual can easily ruin another's career if the second officer is subordinate to the first. In my case, it only took two sentences to become the "kiss of death" for my career. For instance: "In his continuous and zealous effort to produce superior results, Lt. Col. Shouse has, on occasion, allowed his temper to overrule his demonstrated superior ability to make sound decisions, and to direct the efforts of his subordinates. Consequently, these temper flares have impaired his effectiveness in his current position." This was produced and included in one of my Effectiveness Reports by my supervisor, Joe H. Burns.

This occurred when on a trip, my co-pilot refused two direct orders, by me and actually refused to fly unless he got his way concerning food on the way back to our base. Naturally, this was incredulous to me, and I did become angry. However, there was no altercation between the two of us, just words. I reported his actions to both my supervisor and his supervisor, and requested that he be grounded and not allowed to command aircraft on our team trips. This action almost cost this officer his pension, which he was due to receive in six months following his retirement. He would have lost it had I not gone to the General Officer and requested the charges be dropped.

My supervisor, Lt. Col. Burns, whose temper was much more volatile than mine, wrote the Effectiveness Report that virtually ended my career. It is obvious that a personality conflict existed here, and it would appear that Lt. Col. Burns had reached his level of incompetence. Now comes the irony of the whole situation! I was ordered to write my own supervisor's Effectiveness Report by his boss. This report was instrumental in his being promoted to Colonel. That is most definitely against the rules in any military branch! I was transferred out of Burn's control and sent to Germany, for what was to be my last assignment. During my final assignment, I tried desperately to overcome those two sentences that had done me in, but to no avail.

During this last tour of duty, I was stationed at Ramstein Air Base, Germany, which is located near the large city of Kaiserslautern. This city is in the Pfalz section of Germany and located near the border of France and Bavaria. While stationed there, I was the Officer-In-Charge of the transport section of a Special Air Missions Squadron. Our mission was to fly VIP's and Dignitaries throughout Europe and The Middle East. I was Aircraft Commander on many flights into and out of Berlin during the Cold War. My passengers on these trips included His Excellency, Gustav Heinemann, President of West Germany and Willie Brandt, Chancellor of West Germany. These trips, from Koln-Bonn to Berlin, flown in air corridors, occurred when Berlin was located within East Germany and under the watchful eyes of East German Air Force and Russian Fighter Aircraft. Jet aircraft were not allowed to enter Berlin at that time. We were flying Air Force C-118 type aircraft, which is the military counterpart of a DC-6B. These aircraft were old, but well maintained and very plush, by Air Force standards. On occasions, we would have trips to Moscow, the Iron Curtain Countries, Iran, and Israel and throughout the Middle East.

One day, while talking with one of our young pilots, I noticed that he had on a beautiful ring with a red stone and a square and compass on it, which I quickly recognized as being a Masonic emblem. I said to the young man, "You know, I have thought a great deal about that organization-my father was a mason, and I have wondered about how he became one." He looked kinda strange and a bit taken aback. He said, " I think that can be arranged", and he walked away. I thought no more about it until a couple of weeks later when a non-commissioned officer from our base approached me, and said that he understood that I had been asking about the Masonic Lodge. He said that he had a petition, and did I wish to fill it out. I said, "Yes, I think that I would. Let me have it and think about it. So I took the petition home, thought about it a short time, and then filled it out.

Within one to two months, I received a phone call from the non-com that I had spoken to earlier. He asked if I was still interested in the Masonic lodge, and if so, he and two other gentlemen would like to pay a call on me and my wife to talk with us about it. I said that's fine, and we made an appointment for them to come to our house. The evening the three gentlemen came, they were very gracious- they came in, we had coffee and they began to question me as to what I knew about Masonry-which, was just about nothing. I knew that my father had been a Mason in his younger years, but I was unsure if he was still active when he died. But I knew that he did not attend the lodge meetings. My uncle was a Past Master of the Lodge, and most of the influential men where I grew up were Masons. I personally knew several men who were Masons, and had even talked with one of my brothers some six months earlier. We had causally mentioned the Masonic Lodge, and were interested in looking into it. But we took no further action. The gentle-men asked me questions about character, and I learned later that they had run a character reference check on me, asking questions of many people, i.e. what type of person I was, was I trustworthy, etc. They asked my wife how she felt about the Masonic Lodge, and she said that she felt fine about it, and had no problem with it. She could support it, if I were interested in it; it held no problem for her.

Chapter Two
A Search For Light Begins

Following the visit by the three gentlemen, some time later, I received a notice to appear at a Masonic Lodge in Kaiserslautern, Germany, for the conferring of the First Degree upon me...the ENTERED APPRENTICE DEGREE. The first lesson that I learned in Masonry was that all degrees cost dearly. Each degree conferred on a candidate must be paid in advance, and they are not cheap, by any means. Anyway, I appeared at the lodge at the appointed time, along with two other gentlemen. We were teased somewhat about having to ride a goat, and were given very strange clothing to wear. They required us to remove our clothing and everything that was metallic in nature. We donned the special clothing that was provided for this particular degree. Before entering the lodge, I was 'hoodwinked' or blind-folded, and had no idea of what was happening or about to happen. Need I say that I was considerably unnerved, scared out of my wits, for the fear of the unknown is real, indeed. Needless to say, I stumbled through this degree, understanding very little of what had occurred. I was aware of swearing, on the Bible, a very hideous oath if I ever attempted to reveal the secrets of Freemasonry. I was asked, "In whom do you put your trust?" I was prompted to answer "GOD". I was asked what I desired. Again I was cued to answer "Light". Then the blindfold was removed, and I saw the men of the lodge lined up in a particular way and making peculiar signs call 'due guards'. I was congratulated by the men of the lodge, and returned home where I quickly told my wife, "I should have done this many years ago. This takes good men and makes them better."

During this first visit to the lodge, I was told that not one single thing about the lodge would interfere with my religious belief or faith. It would in no way violate my religion nor conflict with my religion because Masonry was <u>NOT</u> a religion. It used many symbols, many of religious origin, and many that came from other origins that I would learn about later. Anyway, I quickly began my memory work. Each time that my wife and I went visiting, I would silently go over my memory work while she practiced her meditation. A great deal of memory work is required in Masonry, and I was coached by a Masonic Brother who was a non-commissioned officer at Ramstein Air Base. He assisted me and within a month, I returned proficiency on the first degree. This meant that I was now eligible to have the second degree conferred upon me.

Within a month, I was again told to report to the lodge at a certain time and date. I was again prepared in a certain way. I entered the lodge again blindfolded, and the Second Degree of Freemasonry was conferred upon me. This is known as the FELLOWCRAFT Degree. Again, I applied myself diligently and began to study harder and harder. Within a month, I returned proficiency on the Second Degree and was now ready for the Third Degree. This degree is known as the Sublime Degree of Master Mason. I was told that I would be <u>raised</u> to that degree on a certain time and date. Being raised to the third degree was a literal term.

In the lodge, there is a legend of one Hiram Abiff, who was supposedly the chief architect of King Solomon's Temple. This, of course, is not true and is indeed, a legend. Freemasonry had its birth in England in the 1700's. Yet, in the third degree, I had to act out the part of Hiram, suffer death at the hands of ruffians, be buried, and then raised from the dead by the Master of the Lodge. Again, I was prepared under similar circumstances as before and went through the ritual.

It was during these three degrees that I took upon myself what was referred to as 'Obligations'. They were, out and out, bloody oaths, sworn on the Bible, curses called down upon myself if I ever revealed the secrets of Freemasonry. This did not bother me at that time, because I thought that it was silly, but once I gave my word, I was not going to go back on it. But why were these things so protected? Many explanations were given to me. For instance; it was to keep certain types of individuals out of the lodge; it was to keep the lodge membership of a certain caliber person- even to the point of keeping certain races out. Again, I was told that Freemasonry began with the building of King Solomon's

Temple in Jerusalem. And of the temple that he built for the people of the Jewish Faith. This was a bald-faced lie!

I must in all fairness, admit that I did enjoy meeting with the men of the lodge, with whom I found myself associating more and more. Within one month of having the third degree conferred upon me, I returned proficiency on this degree, which did take quite a bit of time and effort. It was at this time that I realized my mind was better than I had thought it was when it came to memory work. Nevertheless, upon returning proficiency, the very night that I gave my proficiency test on the third degree, the Master of the Lodge addressed me and gave me an assignment to learn a portion of the third degree and to serve on a degree team that would travel around the country of Germany and Europe, from time to time, and confer these degrees on candidates. The lodge that I was in was part of the American-Canadian Grand Lodge, composed primarily of military people, and it followed the grand Lodge Ritual of the State of Colorado. In many states of the Union, the rituals vary slightly, but they all have the same theme. I was highly motivated, hot-to-trot and up to my ears in Freemasonry.

I remember sending word to a minister in one particular church to get off the Masonic kick and quit criticizing and preaching against masons. "You do not know what you are talking about. Unless you have been a mason, you do not know what you're doing, you don't know what you are criticizing, and you do not really know what masons believe or what they practice. And, for your information, masonry does <u>not</u> conflict with my religious beliefs in any way, shape, or form!" Later, I would learn just how deceived I really was.

Upon receiving the third degree in masonry, I heard that there was a man who lived in the small village where I lived, who was a jeweler on the side, in his home. I paid a visit to this gentleman, and he listened to my request for a Masonic ring. He asked if I had any rings at home. I said, "Yes, I have a High School class ring that is rather old." I brought the ring to him; he looked it over carefully, and said this is perfect. I can set a stone in it. I will cut the top off and set an Onyx in it and put a square and compass in the stone of 24K nugget gold. I also took him my fourteen-degree ring, which looked like a wide wedding band, and had him inscribe inside it my name, date of receipt, etc. I left the ring with the German gentleman and asked if he required a deposit. He said, "No, I don't think one will be required," and he promptly shook my hand. This really shook me up, because it was the first time I had ever received a Masonic handshake outside the lodge.

I followed the instructions of the Worshipful Master of the Lodge and learned the assignment. As expected, I was promptly put on a degree team. During our travels around Europe, we went to the City of Worms, Germany, where the 'EDICT OF DEATH' was issued against Martin Luther when he was excommunicated from the Roman Catholic Church. I really enjoyed the degree work and the fellowship with my Masonic Brothers, but I found that I was drinking more alcohol than usual. It seemed that following the work at the lodges, we would stop at some small tavern. On some occasions, I got rather polluted and on others, I went home higher than a kite!

Not completely satisfied, I began to question other Masonic Brothers about moving up higher in the Masonic structure. Yet, before I got to that point-one month after I had returned proficiency or two months after I had received the third degree as a Master Mason, and now allowed to wear Masonic Emblems, I conferred the Second Degree on two gentlemen, where I served as the Master of the Lodge. On this occasion, the Grand Master of the American-Canadian Grand Lodge was sitting in the East with me. This was indeed, a great Masonic honor. I believe that I did a credible job in the conferring of the degrees.

Anyway, I petitioned the Scottish Rite Council for the further advancement in Masonry, from the third degree to the thirty-second degree. I was able to do this in three solid days in Wiesbaden, Germany. These degrees came so hard and fast, I could hardly remember one item out of each degree. Many of them required the candidate to take on 'obligations' or oaths. These degrees were put on and acted out by masons. These degrees involved great pomp and splendor, and they were very impressive to say the least! I picked up a few books on masonry, especially, <u>MORALS AND DOGMA</u> by Albert Pike. Yet, I never really devoted myself to the study of these books and paraphernalia. Having successfully reached my first goals, I decided to go for the fun part of masonry, which is the Shrine.

I paid my initiation fee into both the Scottish Rite and the Shrine. In June 1975, I was initiated into the Royal Mystic Shrine as a Mystic Noble. I was not at all impressed with this initiation, was disgusted with it, and thought that it was simply, silly! I felt that the ceremony was not dignified, was beneath the conduct of mature, grown men, and was plain, out and out silly! For instance, I was required to wear a ball and chain for twenty-four hours, as well as do many other ridiculous things. However, I proudly donned my fez with its long tassel, and promptly forgot most of the initiation into the Shrine. I had just learned quite a bit, and I kept running into masons in the oddest places. People of high rank in the Air Force, very notable people in Germany, and while traveling around the country, I went by a lodge in Berlin known as 'The Lodge of the Three Lanterns'. Fredrick the Great had been a member of this lodge! WOW! I was traveling in tall cotton and on very high levels for a little boy like me from the hills of Northeast Mississippi.

In July 1975, I was transferred from Germany back to Norton AFB, San Bernardino, California, for processing out of the Air Force under retirement after twenty-two years, fifteen days in the USAF. After settling in Southern California, I immediately found a Blue Lodge, which is a lodge of the three basic degrees, and is common terminology for a local lodge. I began attending the lodge regularly, and petitioned for membership there. This made me a dual member in Germany and California.

Up to this time in my dealings with the Masonic community, I was completely convinced that everything was fine, and in no way was there interference with my Faith or Religion. At that time I was a wayward member of the Church of Christ, had been a member for about thirty years, but did not attend church regularly. My wife and I were not members of the same church, so we did not attend church together; consequently, I did not go alone, either. Since my religious involvement was very little, I was robbing GOD and giving nothing to him. I did not give GOD credit for my presence on Earth or for protecting and preserving me through many close brushes with death. I had lived through so many tough things and hair-raising scrapes. I merely attributed my life to my own doing and my own good luck! That is, indeed, a scary frame of mind for any one. For many sundry reasons, I never became active in the Scottish Rite Organization or the Shrine in the United States. The extent of my involvement was in Europe, but I was still an active member, a card-carrying member, and incidentally, I had to pay dues to all four of these organizations to which I belonged. I had numerous Masonic books, the Lambskin Apron, the Fez, the Cornet, the Monitors, the Jewelry, and all of this kind of stuff; I had it all! Need I say that I wore my ring proudly?

After living two years in Culver City and Playa Del Rey, California, I decided to return to the South or South West where the pace of living was more to my liking, and what I remembered from my childhood. I took a job in Smyrna, Tennessee, just south of Nashville, with Heil-Quaker Corporation as an Electronics Specialist. In reality, my job was more plant manager than electronics specialist, as the Manager spent much of his time out drumming up new business while I was running the plant.

After my first week at this new job, I was returning home one Saturday afternoon, when blue lights came on in my rear view mirror. I pulled over and when the officer approached, I asked why he stopped me. At the time, I was just outside the city of Smyrna and was doing 55 mph. The officer was quite curt since I questioned him, and promptly wrote me a ticket for speeding in a 45 mph zone, having no valid driver's license, and improper registration on my vehicle. I had both California license plates and a California Driver's license. I had only lived in Smyrna for one week. The officer, gleefully, informed me that the minute I was employed in Tennessee, I had to have both license plates and driver's license issued by the state of Tennessee. I was a bit unhappy with this state of affairs, so as he said to me,

"I'll see you in court". I replied, "I rather doubt that". On Monday morning at 6 a.m., I presented myself to the Mayor of Smyrna, who was also the owner of an automobile dealership. I gave him the ticket and flashed my Masonic ring. I had heard that he was a mason. He promptly tore the ticket up, and threw it in the trash while saying, " That officer knows better than this!" The thought hit me; the benefits of this organization are very good. That ticket would have cost me more than one hundred dollars!

Later, I was offered a job in Sturgis, Kentucky, in March 1980. I quickly took it-subsequently moving to Madisonville, Kentucky. The new job was with Pyro Mining Company, a coalmine, where my position was Employee Relations Manager. I made no bones about the fact that I was a mason. I boasted about it, and was very proud to be in my new position. I talked up masonry to many members of the company staff, and asked why so few of them were masons. I never found out why. Even in this new location, I did not demit from any of the lodges that I held membership in or try to transfer my membership to inactive status. I just kept paying the dues. I was having a very difficult time, struggling with a job that was backbreaking and staggering in its intensity. Gradually, my life took a new turn that had me guessing, what's next?

Chapter Three
Education The Hard Way

Somewhere near the first of April 1983, two of my own grown daughters came from Texas to visit me. I was divorced at the time and lived in a large house in Madisonville, Kentucky. My daughters brought three of my grandchildren to visit me and spend about ten days. This was great. I enjoyed my daughters and their children; it was like old times, and we laughed and talked and laughed and talked some more. One day, a new subject entered our conversations. This subject involved BAPTISM IN THE HOLY SPIRIT and speaking in tongues. This was something that I did not believe in one bit! I never had believed in it, though I had witnessed it for myself, and I had been taught, in church, that this phenomenon no longer occurred in religion. That it all was a figment of someone's imagination. It was a taboo subject—you had to stay away from those things. I related to my daughters that a friend of mine from childhood had come by to visit one time, and related a strange tale of something that had happened to her some years before. She was a member of the Baptist Church, and had received the Baptism in the HOLY SPIRIT in the state of Illinois, where she lived at the time. This had come about through the 'Jesus Freaks' or the hippie movement. It became known as the Charismatic Renewal that occurred simultaneously in the Roman Catholic Church and the Episcopal Church. This outpouring of spiritual gifts, the Charismatic Renewal, started to appear in the United States in the late 1960's or early 1970's. I was somewhat curious, and tried to question her more deeply about the experience, but she only kept saying it was too great, and she couldn't put it into words very well. She mentioned something about it being joy unspeakable, which meant nothing to me. By means of sensible explanation, I got very little from this lady.

After relating this to my daughters, they quickly threw me a bomb! At this point, my eldest daughter informed me that she had received the Baptism in question and had spoken in tongues. Upon dropping this little grenade, my younger daughter quickly excused herself and left the room. I learned that they had been praying for a year, about how to break this news to me. Now they expected my explosion, at any minute! They just knew that I would not believe them or would try to convince them that it had never happened. Apparently, I was beginning to learn things about myself from my own children-how dogmatic I was-how unyielding and narrow-minded, and not only impulsive, but dogmatic to the extent that there was no way but my way! WOW!

While keeping myself under control, I questioned them on how this came about. Again, I was confronted with this Charismatic Renewal thing, and I began to wonder if there really was something to this.

One day during the visit of my kiddoes, I went to the store for a few things. My oldest daughter asked me to get a small bottle of olive oil while I was in the store. I did, and very promptly forgot about it. I thought it had something to do with the children. The visit came to an end and my daughters returned to Texas. We had a pleasant visit, and I had enjoyed being with them immensely. This was my first opportunity to sit and chat with them and carry on a conversation with them on a level that I had never been able to before. I thought long and hard on this Baptism thing, and even visited a friend in the city of Morganfield, Kentucky, to discuss this subject. We talked at length and this lady said to me, "Jim, if there is more to Christianity than what I have, I want it, and I'm going to find out if there is more."

At that time I didn't necessarily agree. While mulling these things over in my mind, I recalled an instance in California while I lived there. In 1976, I lived in Playa Del Rey, California, with my daughter, the eldest who had graduated from high school and was working in Los Angeles prior to entering college. A niece of mine, during a short visit, gave me a book that she had read and was somewhat impressed by, the title of which was <u>A NEW SONG</u> by Pat Boone. In this book, Pat described his experience in a similar vein. He had been a member of the Church of Christ for many years, and had somehow become involved in the Baptism of the Holy Spirit along with his wife and his daughters. I read that book with somewhat of a skeptical viewpoint or attitude, and yet, there was a seed of doubt planted in my mind about it, because I had many friends who had experienced this. One thing I did know, I was curious, and I knew without a doubt, that my daughters would not lie to me, and that they knew what they were telling me. Not only was I in a quandary over this subject, I noticed that things began to happen in my house that I had not experienced before, at least, knowingly. I had lived alone many times, having been assigned to very remote locations, and due to other problems that cropped up from time to time. I was alone quite often, and there were times when I really enjoyed being alone, having my own solitude and doing my own thing.

I have always tried to keep from bothering other people or getting on their nerves. But still, living alone leaves a lot to be desired because man was not meant to be alone. That is why woman was created, to be a companion and mate for us guys. Anyway, things began to happen in my household for which I found no explanation.

Chapter Four
A Search For Real Light & Truth

Some time ago, someone said, "Silence is golden". I learned that silence can be deafening at times. My household took on a distinct difference from the norm. Noises began to get my attention that I had never noticed before. At that time in my life, I was living much faster than ever before. I had just gone through a divorce, and was drinking more than usual for me; however, I was not an alcoholic or even approaching that stage. I was just drinking regularly, which for me was to excess. I had little to do at home, living alone, and drinking was an escape from the worries that plagued me. The stress at work was heavy and nerve racking to say the least. My job involved writing all company policies and organizing and developing all company benefits. For the first three years on this job, I averaged twelve hours per day, and since I was on salary, there was no overtime pay. I also helped my boss fly the company plane, for which I was not paid one cent. My boss and I split up flying duties and spent our weekends picking up dignitaries at sundry places. The company seemed to think that pilots loved flying so much that they would give up all free time to engage in blasting off into the wild blue yonder.

I realized just how empty and barren my life had become, and I knew that my spiritual condition was in sad shape. I was aware that I was searching for something, yet I could not put my finger on the subject in question or find any answers to my dilemma. I searched throughout my work for answers that failed to materialize. I pestered my friends and sought for answers that did not come. I searched within Freemasonry and found no answers. Of all answers that came, none fulfilled the emptiness that I felt. Something was missing from my life, and it wasn't the fact that I was single. I felt a yearning that I could not put my finger on.

Then the things started to happen in my house for which I could find no logical explanation. I was sitting in my den one Sunday afternoon watching a football game, when I heard my front door open and someone came in. The person walked through my dining room, and approached the den where I was sitting. I looked up, expecting to see someone. There was no one to be seen! I merely thought that someone was playing tricks on me. My house was carpeted, so I did not hear footsteps, I felt the floor vibrate as the steps progressed to the den. The way that my house was constructed, a 200 pound man could walk across the floor, and you could feel it, if you were sitting quietly, without saying a word or making a sound. When this happened, I got up, went into the dining room, because I was sure that someone was there. I found no one and the door was still closed. I returned to the den and sat down again.

Shortly thereafter, the same sounds began again, and I experienced the same thing all over again. This happened more times than I like to remember. Finally, one day I determined to just ignore this phenomenon and go on about my business. This time I felt the presence of some one or something, for the hair on the back of my neck stood on end and the hair on my arms did also. Chills went up and down my spine in an unnerving manner. My skin began to crawl and I said out loud, "What is happening?" The minute that I got up to see what was happening, there would be silence and not a sound heard. Need I say that I was becoming a bit unnerved, not frightened, just unnerved? I finally realized that I was encountering something strange and invisible, but something whose presence I could sense.

It was about this time when my friend in Morganfield called and said "Jim, I am going to Indianapolis to meet George Otis, President of High Adventure Ministries, Bible Voice, and who was installing short wave radio stations all over the world. These stations broadcast nothing but music and scripture readings around the clock. This man, a previous Vice-President of Lear Jet, had discovered the missing link in his life, and had written numerous books on several topics concerning Christianity. In his first book, HIGH ADVENTURE, George explains how he had an encounter with GOD, THE HOLY SPIRIT. My dear friend indicated to me that she was going to find out if this was real or not. I wanted to go with her, but I had weekend guests and could not. I told her to please call me upon her return and describe what happened. She assured me that she would. She drove to Indianapolis on Friday evening and expected to return on Sunday. I heard nothing from her, so at about nine p.m. Sunday, I called her. She walked in the door as the phone was ringing. I immediately asked her, " What happened?" She was laughing and crying at the same time. I found this strange because I had never heard her cry before. I had heard her laughter many times, but this was different. She said, "Jim, you have no idea what GOD has in store for you." I said, " Then come over here and tell me, please." She came to my house, which was forty two miles from her home, after having driven from Indianapolis, Indiana, that day. She laughed and cried and tried to explain the unexplainable- trying to put into words an experience that she had felt but which is impossible to describe. I really began to think that I had been wrong about this thing called Baptism In The Holy Spirit. I began to seek for answers that had eluded me in the past. I finally turned to the Bible and began to read, search, seek, and ask. I found a scripture for which I had paid little attention in the past or for which I had some other answer.

This scripture found in LUKE 11: 9-13, hit me like a ton of bricks: "So I say to you, ask, and it will be given to you; seek and you will find; knock and it will be opened to you." "For everyone who asks receives, and he who seeks, finds, and to him who knocks, it will be opened." "If a son asks for bread from any father among you, will he give him a stone?" "Or if he asks for a fish, will he give him a serpent instead of a fish?" "Or if he asks for an egg, will he offer him a scorpion?" " IF YOU THEN, BEING EVIL, KNOW HOW TO GIVE GOOD GIFTS TO YOUR

CHILDREN, HOW MUCH MORE WILL YOUR HEAVENLY FATHER GIVE THE <u>HOLY SPIRIT</u> TO THOSE WHO ASK HIM!" In the past, I had looked at this scripture very superficially, and had taken it only on its surface. With my daughter's and my dear friend's testimonies, I knew that I had been wrong. You see, I had been taught against this belief. I was told that the age of miracles was long past, and the laying on of hands and the Baptism in The Spirit was a thing of the past.

All this ended with the death of the Apostle John in approximately 97 A.D. I called my dear friend and said to her, "Please, help me." "Unusual things are happening to me that I can neither explain nor describe. I now believe that the Baptism in the Holy Spirit is real, and I want it." She told me that she would call me back. The next day, while at work, she called me and said, "be at my house tomorrow evening. We will be going to a praise service." I asked what a praise service was, but she said you will find out after we get there. I went to my friend's house, as directed, and then later to the home of Jerry Manning, who lives in Morganfield.

We went to his house about six p.m. as; the service was to begin at seven p.m. I explained why I was there, and that I wanted to be baptized in the HOLY SPIRIT. He questioned me at length about my beliefs, what I had practiced all my life, if I had read the scriptures, and why I was making this request. He read several scriptures and said, "We must pray." I repeated a prayer after him, wherein I renounced the occult and all of the works of the powers of darkness. I had never prayed with such fervor in my life! The people there laid their hands upon me, and I felt peace like I had never felt before. I was told to open my mouth and speak in a new language. I opened my mouth but nothing came out; not a sound. For some reason, I was not disturbed by this development. I had gone for several days without sleep, and I was completely exhausted. Jerry reassured me that I had, indeed, received the Baptism in The Holy Spirit, and to believe it. I did.

Rather than return to my home in Madisonville, I went to my friend's house and lay down on the couch to sleep. I was very tired and sleepy but, just before I dozed off, I looked at the ceiling- lo and behold- I saw a face appear on the ceiling. The face had white hair, cut in a roman haircut, and had a neatly trimmed white mustache and beard. The face had no expression. It just looked straight ahead- no smile- no frown. I remember saying, "Lord, I wonder if that's you"...then I promptly fell asleep.

The next day, I found myself walking about twelve inches above the ground. At least, that was the way I felt! It began to dawn on me that I had, indeed, received the Baptism that I had sought. I felt the power of The SPIRIT like I had never felt before. That description found in the Bible of 'joy unspeakable' is very true and accurate in ever detail. Feelings experienced are extremely difficult to express in terms familiar to us. There are things that are beyond what we know or can express. For a period of at least three weeks, I was on a spiritual high. I loved and I felt loved. My first known feeling was something very hard to describe...I felt GOD loving me! I have felt the emotion of loving someone else, but I had never physically felt someone loving me before. I saw a large spotlight placed on JESUS CHRIST. Again, I felt loved by FATHER, SON, and HOLY SPIRIT. I <u>knew</u> that JESUS was alive and seated at the right hand of the FATHER. I <u>knew</u> that Jesus had all power and authority. I no longer just believed it and mentally accepted it - -<u>I KNEW IT!</u> What a difference! I also found something that I had never experienced before in my life- I could not keep my mouth closed. I wanted to tell everyone how wonderful it was, and what a wonderful experience I had. It seemed imperative that I tell everyone just how much they were missing in their lives. I tried to explain how my life had gone from just existing to really living. I had found 'the abundant life'. WOW! All these feelings, experiences and emotions that I now felt, yet were so difficult to express sensibly, - these were all new to me. I felt love for others- - a different kind of love, a forgiving love, an all-encompassing love.

The next day, I got on the phone, and called my oldest daughter in Abilene, Texas. I tried to explain to her what had happened, that is, I had received the Baptism in the Holy Spirit, just as we had discussed previously, when she had visited me. My daughter said, "Dad, I have a confession to make to you." Do you remember the olive oil that I had asked you to buy at the store when I was there?" I said yes. She said, "Before I left your house, I anointed every doorpost and every window, and I prayed THAT THE INHABITANTS OF THIS HOUSE WOULD BE FILLED WITH THE HOLY SPIRIT." Two weeks after her actions, my daughter's prayer was answered and fulfilled! I knew nothing of what she had done, but I knew definitely, that something was going on! In view of my daughter's actions, it appears to me that a messenger of the Lord, an angel, was present in my house and was bringing pressure to bear on me to take action of my own. I definitely know that the 'Super natural' was present. Too many things had happened that were unexplainable.

I have never been an emotional person, but have been one who dwelt on logic. My degree in General Education has a major in Mathematics, a minor in Physics- - two and two had always been four to me.

The Super-natural was always within my imagination, but only in my imagination! I immediately went to my home state of Mississippi to visit my family, who are all church members. I told them that we have been wrong all these years concerning this subject. I tried, in my inept way to explain what had happened to me, and that I could not keep my mouth shut on the subject, and for the first time in my life, I approached my older brother about coming to Jesus Christ- claiming him as Lord and Savior, believing on Him. I had power to witness like I had never before, just as is recorded in the first chapter of the book of ACTS in the New Testament. After the Holy Spirit came upon the Apostles, Jesus told them that they would be witnesses for HIM throughout Jerusalem, Judea, Samaria, and to the uttermost parts of the Earth. I could not be quiet! I had to tell everyone.

People at work began to ask, "What has happened to Jim?" One day, my assistant, while driving with me to Madisonville, KY, asked me bluntly what had happened to me. I asked if he was really interested, and after he said that he was, I told him to fasten his seat belt; then, I told him. He showed very little reaction. I took it as skepticism, and that he didn't know what to say or think. Then it dawned on me. You don't speak Chinese to someone who doesn't understand the Chinese language. My experience was SPIRITUAL, and one doesn't speak spiritual things to unspiritual people!

One week after these events, I picked up the phone and dialed George Otis in Van Nuys, California, at the VOICE OF HOPE MINISTRIES. I called to thank him for a book that he had sent me; THE THUNDER OF HIS POWER. During our conversation, George mentioned that he was aware that I had received the Baptism in The Holy Spirit, and he asked if I had received a prayer language, or the gift of tongues. I told him that I had not received this gift, and that I was not concerned about it, and that the Lord knows this, and will give me this gift whenever HE wants me to have it. He said to me, "Close the door to your office, Jim, for we need to pray." I answered, "George, I'm at work." He said, "So am I; now close the door to your office." So, I closed the door, and George began to lead us in prayer. After he finished, he told me to open my mouth and praise GOD in a different language, that is, one other than English. Every time I opened my mouth, only English came out. He chided me and said, "No, I said a language other than English." I first began to babble, but before long another language began to roll. George said one word, "Magnificent," and hung up the phone.

I went out, got into my car and drove five miles to the next town. I said, "LORD, if this is real please keep it up." I kept speaking all kinds of syllables that were new to me. Later, I discovered some of the words that I had said in the Bible. Believe me, that got my attention, big time! I had been speaking Hebrew, without knowing one word other then Shalom.

However, I must add that I do not have the gift of speaking in tongues, that is one of the gifts of the Holy Spirit. HE gives his gifts severally, as he wishes, and all are for the build-up of the Church of Our Lord. They are not given for show or to be used as one sees fit. Anyway, I found that most people with whom I shared this experience, looked upon me as one having an air of holier-than-thou. Yet, I can truthfully say that my zeal was mistaken for self-righteousness. My desires to share GOD and his gifts with my fellow man was met with rebuff. These people would ask me, " Do you think that you have something that other Christians do not have?" The only answer that I could give was. "I don't know, but if I do, it is so great that you ought to have it too."

Strange, following this experience; this great, great experience, I was brought crashing to the ground while trying to make restitution for wrongs done by me in the past. On one such attempt, I spoke to a lady who suggested that maybe my experiences were not from God, but from the other direction. This unnerved me to no end, for it was perilously close to Blaspheming the Holy Spirit, which, according to our Lord in the New Testament is the Unpardonable Sin. That is serous business in anyone's book! Nevertheless, I did try to right all known wrongs done by me that I could remember. Finally, I had, indeed, found true light and the only real truth. How very enlightening!

Chapter Five
The Madisonville Horror

After having experienced all these wonderful events and feeling like a new and different person, surely, I thought, now I will live happily ever after and life will be a breeze. Not so! The strange events that happened within my house now took on a different and more drastic nature! Now, instead of merely getting my attention, they seemed to be harassing me. For instance, sleep became a very difficult and elusive thing. Once, I was sitting in my kitchen in the middle of the afternoon, reading, and here came the footsteps again. They seemed to begin in another room, and then proceeded to where I was sitting. Incidentally, I lived alone at the time, since I had become divorced. The steps would come into the kitchen, approach my chair, and I could feel the presence of the being, whoever or whatever it was. At this point, I did not know whether the being was good or evil. In explaining this to one minister, he said, "GOD is not the author of confusion, but of peace." I Cor. 14:33, "So therefore, Jim, this must not be from GOD." I slowly began to consider the possibility that this being was not a good spirit, but an unclean one. The incidents began to accelerate, and I began to react to them.

On several occasions, the being would approach me while I was watching television in my den, come right up to my chair, and my chair would move and almost turn over. My hair would stand up on my head, neck, and arms. My skin would crawl, and I would feel severe fear. This feeling went from the top of my head to the bottom of my feet. Later, as these episodes continued, this fear turned into stark terror. If you have ever sat in a room alone with your eyes closed, and felt someone enter, you could physically feel their presence, but without fear. You did not fear them; for chances are that you knew who it was. In my case. I felt the presence of this being, but great fear-involuntary fear-would come upon me. I did the only thing that I knew to do in this case, and that was to demand, in the name of JESUS CHRIST, that the being leave and not return! Upon doing this, there would be silence for a few minutes. But the very minute that I began to doze or take a nap, here we would go again.

In retrospect, I began to realize that it appeared that the name of JESUS did not have any effect. This in itself was a lie! And I knew it, for I know the power of HIS name, the power of the risen CHRIST. So I went through a period of confusion; wondering why these incidents kept occurring. Incidentally, I was not drinking during these events, for following the Baptism in The Holy Spirit, I poured all my booze down the drain. I no longer needed it, and in fact, didn't want it. So, I couldn't blame this on alcohol or on DTs. I simply could not explain this to anyone, including myself. I went to an Episcopal priest, told him about my plight, and it appeared to me that he thought that I had flipped my wig. He just told me to stop reading the book of Revelation in the Bible. Strange, for I hadn't been reading anything from the Bible.

I even went to a farmer in Union County, Kentucky, for I knew that he was Charismatic and had experienced some strange things. After listening to me, he said, "Jim, what are you afraid of?" I answered, "Satan!" The reason that I feared Satan was that I mistakenly had applied the scripture, Matthew 10:28, to him rather than to GOD. For the scripture says, "And do not fear those who kill the body but cannot kill the soul. But rather fear HIM who is able to destroy both body and soul in hell." For many years, I had mistakenly applied this scripture to Satan. However, during my visit with my oldest daughter, she had told me, "Dad, that is talking about GOD". HE is the only one who can do that".

Later, in my own study of the scriptures, I discovered that she was right. Anyway, this farmer said to me, "Jim, why are you putting up with this?" I said, "I'm not just putting up with it; I'm trying everything that I know to do, and that's why I am here asking you." He said, "I think that you have a Poltergeist in your house. I knew that a Poltergeist was a German word for a noisy ghost. All my life, I had been led to believe that there is no such thing as a ghost. He said, "Stand on faith, demand that the spirit leave, and <u>stand on faith</u>."

I did as he instructed. It would produce peace and quiet, and then after only a few minutes, it would start all over again. It never dawned on me that demons rarely ever work or travel alone; they are in a pack and if one is cast out, another replaces him, so as to give the appearance that the casting out has not worked and that there is no power in the name of JESUS CHRIST! One must keep driving them out! I have been talking on the phone in my kitchen during the day, and would have to lay the phone down and take care of the interruption; then go on with my conversation. I kept asking myself how a spirit could make footsteps that I could feel and would cause the house to shake or tremble. I still don't know how this happened, for I would think that a spirit would be weightless. Whatever or whoever it was, it certainly knew how to bring terror to me. This did not happen at the stroke of mid-night or the wee hours of the morning, but during the afternoon, in broad daylight. This was not Halloween, it was any day and any time that I was alone. This seemed to occur in my house, only, when I was alone. When others came to visit me, nothing happened so that they noticed. I noticed, however! As one can easily see, I became desperate for sleep. Each evening after going to bed, I had to deal with this problem. I normally would retire at about ten p.m. and rise to go to work at five a.m. I had commuting time of about fifty minutes and had to be at work at 6:30 a.m.

I kept asking over and over again, why, why, why? During this time, I began to think about reuniting my family that had been split by divorce. This seemed to be part of the move to make restitution for wrongs that occurred in the past. I talked to my ex-wife on the phone, and it looked like we might get back together. This occurred in October 1983.

I recalled the scripture that says, "It is not good for man to be alone," from the book of Genesis. This may have had an effect on me, I really don't know. Anyway, the encounters with the supernatural began to accelerate again. There was a banging on the walls, pictures and other objects that were hanging on the walls fell down with a crash. Noises would occur within the house that I had never heard before. Once, I just about convinced myself that the house was settling and that caused noises, but then I had never heard of a house settling with the cadence of footsteps! While watching television, a bloodcurdling scream would come through the speaker that didn't match the program. As I write this chapter my typewriter has started acting strangely. The ribbon keeps tangling and the cartridge acts up. I am determined to complete this account!

These strange things continued to happen and my ability to get sleep was practically non-existent. I began to sleep with the light on. That is, if one can call the dozing that I did as sleep. I found myself beginning to be afraid of the dark. I was afraid of the powers of darkness. But the minute that my eyelids began to close, the footsteps would commence, and I felt the presence of this being in my bedroom. Even with the lights on, this happened. I played tapes of the New Testament around the clock in my house. I also played hymns and spiritual songs-anything to break the silence in that house. Whenever I sensed the being enter my bedroom, I would open my eyes and the movement would stop. As my eyelids drooped, here we go again. I would command it to leave in the name of JESUS CHRIST of Nazareth, and it would seem to leave. At least the tormenting eased up. Incidentally, I really learned the definition of torment, i.e. , terrifying fear.

One night, I had gone to bed at about ten p.m. I had had very little sleep for days. I said my prayers and began to praise GOD. Somewhere I had read that GOD inhabits the praises of his people, Psalm 22:3. Someone had told me that the enemy, Satan, and his helper's cannot stand the praise of GOD. Lying flat on my back in bed, I lifted my hands in the air and began to praise and thank GOD like I never had before. This being may have become angry, for it came to my bed and kicked it. At least that is how it felt to me. I have experienced the feeling of being kicked in the back while in bed through a mattress. You say that's impossible, well I'm here to tell you that it did happen! I do not pretend to know how- - it just happened. Finally, this one particular night, I was very tired and worn. I had gone to bed at about ten p.m., and had wrestled all night trying to get some sleep. At approximately five a.m. the next morning, I gave up fighting and said to myself, " I just can't fight anymore." The next instant after thinking this, I was hit by something that felt like an electric shock. My nerves flinched, my eyelids flicked, my ears popped, as if I were changing altitude, and I tingled all over. Strange. I didn't care about anything anymore. I had no resolve to fight or put up resistance. I said, "What's the use?" I just can't fight what I can't see.

The next morning, I got out of bed and went to work as I usually did. And I just did not care about my job or anything else. I went into my office and I believe through the providence of GOD, my secretary stayed out of my way that day. She was my secretary for many years, and is a dear, dear lady. I'm glad that I didn't give her a difficult time. Yet, another employee did come to my office with whom I had worked closely. For some reason, I attacked her verbally with a vehemence that surprised and shocked me. Venom spit from my mouth, and I blamed her for all the ills of our office. I was unfair, to say the least, but I just didn't care. I'm glad that nobody challenged me that day or gave me a hard way to go, for I probably would have wound up in a fight or getting fired. This day, I experienced something that I had read about, but never expected to learn first hand. I had an out-of-body experience. No, I have never smoked pot or taken any drugs of a 'recreational' nature, only those prescribed by a doctor. I remember standing over in the corner of my office, and looking at myself sitting there at my desk. I heard the words coming out of my mouth, and suddenly it dawned upon me. That is not my voice! It was my body, but not my voice. Strange! Nevertheless, I was filled with venom that day.

After going through the wonderful experience that I had, while attending church in Madisonville, a comment had been made by a lady that she hoped I would not split the church with my beliefs and experiences. I called this lady and told her in no uncertain terms that she need not worry about me splitting that church, for I never intended to go there anymore. And I didn't. I was so full of venom that day that it only seemed natural to snap at everyone. I was amazed at how easy it was. I was amazed at myself. Since I felt especially vindictive that day, I picked up the phone and dialed my ex-wife out in Texas. I told her to forget about any wedding, for it was off! She realized that something was wrong, but did not know that I was under severe spiritual attack. A war seemed to be going on within me! She said to me, "Put on the Christian armor," I said, "I am sick and tired of hearing that. Tell me how to do just that." I have never met anyone who could tell me how to don the armor. No human had ever explained that in a way that I could understand or follow. Later on, a time came when GOD told me how, and I quickly wrote it down.

The workday finally ended, and I got in my car and started driving home. A thought came into my mind, what now? I remembered that while on the phone to Texas, my oldest daughter got on the phone, she sensed that something was drastically wrong, and she began to pray for me and with me. In her prayer, she touched a nerve within me, and a light of hope began to blink. So, as I was driving home that evening, another thought hit me: you know what you must do! I said, "Yes, I know what I must do. I opened my mouth to pray, and it was as if someone or something put hands around my throat and closed off my voice box. I could not get anything to come out. I tried again and again and finally, I got one word out-JESUS. Immediately, I was released, and the being that had been with me all day vanished. My emotions ran the gamut! My heart broke, my eyes flooded with tears, and I wept in praise to GOD. The relief that I felt was too intense to describe coherently.

After arriving at home, I was put on the defensive again, because the attacks and the tormenting were still there. One night I left my house and went to a motel in Madison-ville. The problem went with me. The same footsteps were with me and the same sleeplessness was there, too. Once, a minister came to talk with me. He made it very clear that my style of living was the cause of all my problems. I pointed out to him that of the twenty-seven books and letters of the New Testament, some twenty-one of them were written to churches and Christians, telling them how to live the Christian life, and therein are listed many things that they were doing that were not acceptable to our LORD. I'm just a human and a sinner. I suffered temptation like I never had before, that I could remember. The minister didn't help me, and if anything, he discouraged me.

Finally, I left my house in the Scanfield Subdivision of Madisonville, Kentucky, and moved to a motel in Sullivan, Kentucky. This motel was immediately behind the building, in which I worked. I remained there for a week. I was desperately in need of sleep, and for some reason, I had peace there. On Sunday morning, after this week, I got up and went to church in a small town in Illinois named Shawneetown. This is just across the Ohio River from Sturgis, Kentucky. The Church was non-denominational, and I witnessed the ordination of a young man and his wife into the ministry of the Lord Jesus Christ. The Holy Spirit began to urge me to go forward and encourage the young couple. A dear friend with whom I was sitting, told me later that it was obvious that HE was leading me. I left that church and became very angry....angry that a being had driven me out of my own house, and forced me into a motel. I drove back to my house determined to make a stand and not budge an inch! I went throughout the house, anointed every doorpost and window, and prayed that the house would be dedicated to THE ALMIGHTY GOD. I demanded and commanded all of Satan's agents to depart and never reenter. My monologue included, "I will not leave again, this is my property, and the very worst thing that could happen to me is the destruction of my physical body. My soul and spirit belong to GOD. I will no longer fear you, Satan, for now, I only fear GOD. Lo and behold, the attacks began to ease up. What blessed relief!

CHAPTER SIX
LIGHT OVERCOMES DARKNESS

One Sunday evening, while visiting in a friend's home, the young man whose ordination I had witnessed said to me, "Jim, what is that thing on your hand?" I said, "Oh, do you mean my Masonic ring?" he replied, "Yes. That should come off. Don't you know that light has no fellowship with darkness, and it is wrong for you to be in that organization." I didn't entirely agree, but a seed of doubt was planted in my mind that would later come to fruition through study and research. I began to study and do some research in about July 1983. About this time, I was invited to a small town in Missouri to speak to a group of people who all lived on a farm. They had a service on Saturday night that began at seven p.m. and ended at about mid-night. I was invited to speak at this service, in fact, I was bursting to speak about my experiences. During this short visit, a lady advanced in age, said to me, "Brother, what is that thing on your hand?" I answered, "Do you mean my Masonic ring?" She said, "Don't you know what you have done?" I said, "No, as far as I know I joined the Masonic Lodge, and it had nothing to do with my religion or faith." She handed me a book and an audiotape. The book was <u>Should a Christian be a Mason</u> by E.M. Storms, and was endorsed by a minister in Florida who had been a 33rd degree Mason, and had renounced it. The tape was on the subject of "witchcraft" by John Todd who had come out of it, and had become a Christian. She gave me these two items and said, "This tape is for you alone. Be careful about letting anyone hear it, for we fear for Brother Todd's life, now that he has come out of witchcraft and is now serving Christ." I read the book, and it pointed out some very unusual things that I will discuss later. The book showed me some facts that I did not know, some things that my brother masons had failed to tell me, or they just didn't know these facts themselves.

Albert Pike was the father of Scottish Rite Freemasonry, and wrote a book on Freemasonry entitled, <u>Morals and Dogma</u>. This book was so dry and filled with double talk that I had never bothered to try to read it. One day while I was at a mall shopping for something, I noticed a used book sale going on in the hallway. I have always loved books and like very much to read, so I stopped by and browsed a bit. I would never have believed this, but there on a table was Albert Pike's book. I quickly bought it and started thumbing through it. To my surprise, many of the questions that I had were written by hand in the margin of the pages. It was like I had been led to this table! I could hardly believe my eyes! The margin notes seemed to have anticipated my questions and concerns. As a matter of note, Scottish Rite Freemasonry takes a candidate from the third degree up to and including the 32nd degree. One more degree is allowed, but can only be received as an honor. One that is presented at the Masonic Temple in Washington, D.C. This degree cannot be purchased, but is awarded for exemplary service to the brotherhood. Many presidents have received the 33rd degree; for instance, Harry Truman and Franklin Roosevelt, and I'm sure many others.

As I began to study, I came to realize that all branches of Freemasonry, recognize all religions and cults. Buddha, which is an idol, the Egyptian Sun God, Ra, and many, many other heathen, idolatrous religions. It recognizes Mormonism, Hinduism, and all the other "ISMS" of the world. While one of the great lights of masonry is the Bible, you can also find the Book of Mormon on an altar in a lodge in Utah. One can also find the writings and beliefs of other religious leaders in various countries wherein you might visit a lodge. I have sat in a lodge with men from South Africa, Germany, and many other countries. A friend of mine and I were invited to a lodge in Germany where we watched a degree put on entirely in the German language. Not one word of English was spoken in that lodge.

In my research, I delved deeply into Morals and Dogma, by Albert Pike, the Encyclopedia of Freemasonry, by Albert G. Mackey, The Lost Keys of Freemasonry, by Manly P. Hall, The Royal Masonic Cyclopedia, by Kenneth Mackenzie and many other books as well. What I learned, shook me to the bottom of my sanity. I had been told so many times that Freemasonry was most definitely not a religion. Then in Mackey's Encyclopedia of Freemasonry pages 618 and 619, I found these words, "Masonry is, in every sense of the word, except one, and that its least philosophical, an eminently religious institution- that it is indebted solely to the religious element which it contains for its origin and for its continued existence, and that without this religious element it would scarcely be worthy of cultivation by the wise and good."... "Masonry, then, is indeed, a religious institution; and on this ground mainly, if not alone, should the religious Mason defend it". Then in Pike's book, page 219, he says, "Masonry is the universal, eternal, immutable religion such as GOD planted it in the heart of the universal humanity", then on pages 213, he also says, "Every Masonic Temple is a Temple of Religion, and its teachings, are instructions in religion." Talk about double talk! I, like all masons, were told many lies-we were deceived- simply because we never would have suspected that someone as honorable as masons would deceive us. And we didn't bother to investigate to find out for ourselves! That is a very, easy deception! Being mis-led, mis-guided, while trusting others is one way that the enemy of men's souls works.

Upon listening to the tape by John Todd, while standing before a body of Christians in the Carolinas, he mentioned that any mason who was in the audience and was interested in learning about their initiation into Freemasonry, if they would stand by until he finished, he would compare their initiation into masonry with his initiation into witchcraft. He said that he could match the Masonic initiation word for word with his. THIS GOT MY ATTENTION, BIG TIME! Had I, ignorantly, gotten involved in something as clandestine as witchcraft or sorcery? I knew that the Bible was very explicit on these points. We are to have nothing to do with fortunetellers, mediums, those with familiar spirits, astrology and the like.

In I Samuel the 28th Chapter, we read where King Saul of Israel, went to a witch or medium in the town of En Dor to call back the prophet Samuel from the dead. He wanted to know if he would be victorious over the Philistines the next day in battle. What Samuel said was not what Saul wanted to hear. The next day he would die along with his three sons in the battle, and Israel would be defeated by the Philistines. Grave doubts began to bother me.

What have I done? I have been DECEIVED! Mr. John Todd was born into a family of witches. It is a great delight on Halloween night to dress our little children in ghoulish costumes and send them out trick-or-treating. We play it off and say "Aren't they cute!" We bring attention and glory to the powers of darkness. Witchcraft is real, but most people do not have the wisdom or knowledge to see it, or will not take the time to investigate to see what they are promoting. (For instance, the U.S. Army has a Wiccan Chaplain for those who believe and practice the religion of witchcraft. The Veterans Administration has now approved an emblem for the gravestones of its soldiers who were members of the Wiccan Religion. It is a five-pointed star with a circle around it.)

Mr. Todd claimed that he worshiped Lucifer, and he would never trust any high-ranking Mason. I began to see that if all of these religions claimed equality with Christianity, just where does that put Christ our Lord? Is he only equal to Buddha, Mohammed, or any of the other religious figures listed in History? Did that make Him merely a religious leader or teacher? The Bible teaches that Jesus is the Son of GOD. The Ten Commandments state, "Thou shall have no other Gods before me". I recall that Jesus said in the Gospels that, "Hear O Israel, love the Lord your GOD with all of your heart, soul, strength and mind." Now, if I sit in lodge with a recognition of Joseph Smith on a par equal with Jesus Christ; with Buddha on an equal par with Jesus, or any other religious deity- worshipped and followed by many, many people in this world, would I not be violating my own religion? Would not freemasonry itself be interfering with my beliefs and my religious faith? Could I accept someone on an equal with the Son of GOD Almighty, who created the Universe and all that is in it? Him whom I trust as LORD, KING, AND SAVIOR, I would lower to the rank or standing of Buddha? NO!!! I continued my study and found more things that shocked me and dismayed me to no end!

Chapter Seven
Darkness Flees From Light

I continued my search for the truth concerning Freemasonry, and what I learned made me very uneasy and troubled! I had been told, and I accepted it as the truth, that Freemasonry began with the building of the Temple in Jerusalem by King Solomon. Then to my surprise, I found that it actually began in England in 1717. All the backing in of the various theories proposed to have begun with Buddha as the first legislator were not true! Buddha lived a thousand years before Christ, and masonry was nowhere in the picture. Manly P. Hall, in his book, <u>The Lost Keys of Freemasonry</u> said, "The true Mason is not creed-bound. He realizes with the divine illumination of his lodge that as a Mason his religion must be universal; Christ, Buddha, or Mohammed, the name means little, for he recognizes only the light, and not the bearer. He worships at every shrine, bows before every altar, whether in temple, mosque or cathedral, realizing with his truer understanding, the oneness of all spiritual truth." Pike, says in <u>MORALS AND DOGMA</u>, page 226, "GOD is above all Baalim." The word Baalim, is simply defined as "False GOD or Idol." The Masonic Author also included the God of the Christian in that category! He also said on page 476, "Everything good in nature comes from OSIRIS" (he is the sun god of the Ancient Egyptians) "order, harmony and the favorable temperature for the seasons and celestial periods." As a matter of interest, Osiris was the Egyptian god whose annual death and resurrection personified the self-renewing vitality and fertility of nature.

Take a look at your one-dollar bill, and see the all-seeing eye of Osiris. Masons were instrumental in designing our paper currency. Page 104 and 105 of Pike's book, reads, "Masonry, like all religions, all the Mysteries, Hermeticism, and Alchemy, conceals its secrets from all except the Adepts and Sages, or the Elect, and uses false explanations and misinterpretations of its symbols to mislead those who deserve only to be misled; to conceal the truth, which it calls light, from them, and to draw them away from it." Pike goes on to say on page 819, "The Blue Degrees are but the outer court or portico of the temple. Part of the symbols are displayed there to the initiate, but he is <u>intentionally </u>misled by false interpretations. It is not intended that he shall understand them, but it is intended that he shall imagine he understands them." WOW! Masonic experts even admit that they deceive their own members!

Next, I found what masonry teaches about the Bible. Pike says on Page 105 of his book, "The teachers, even of Christianity, are, in general, the most ignorant of the true meaning if that which they teach. There is no book of which so little is known as the Bible. To most who read it, it is as incomprehensible as the Sohar." Then on pages 744 and 745, Pike writes, "All truly dogmatic religions have issued from the Kabalah and return to it. The Kabalah alone consecrates the Alliance of the Universal Reason and the Divine Word. The Bible, with all the allegories it contains, expresses, in an incomplete and veiled manner only, the religious science of the Hebrews."

The Kabalah is a book of ancient Jewish mysticism and magic! Some scholars say that Solomon wrote the Kabalah, after he had gone off the deep end and followed his wives' heathen gods.

According to masonry, God, as we know him is not the God of masonry. For instance, Manly P. Hall wrote in his book, "When the mason learns that the Key to the warrior on the block is the proper application of the dynamo of living power, he has learned the Mystery of his Craft. The seething energies of LUCIFER are in his hands, and before he may step onward and upward, he must prove his ability to properly apply this energy." Now to make matters even worse, Albert Pike, Grand Commander, Sovereign Pontiff of Universal Freemasonry gave instructions to the Sovereign Grand Inspectors General on July 14,1889. These instructions are, "You may repeat this to the Brethren of the 33rd, 32nd, 31st, and the 30th degrees-the Masonic Religion should be, by all of us initiates of the higher degrees, maintained in the purity of the <u>Luciferian Doctrine</u>. If Lucifer were not God, would Adonay (the God of the Christians) whose deeds prove his cruelty, perfidy and hatred of man, barbarism and repulsion for science, would Adonay and his priests, calumniate him? Yes, Lucifer is God, and unfortunately Adonay is also god. For eternal law is that there is no light without shade, no beauty without ugliness and no white without black. Thus the doctrine of Satanism is a heresy; and the true and pure philosophical religion is the belief in Lucifer, the equal of Adonay; but Lucifer, God of Light and God of Good, is struggling for humanity against Adonay, the God of darkness and Evil." And this garbage will not interfere with my Christian Faith??? How very stupid I once was!

When I was put through the many degrees of the Scottish Rite program, they came so fast and furious, all 29 degrees in a period of three days, I hardly remember much about them. However, in the York Rite Program, A section called the Royal Arch Mason, the candidate is asked, "Brother Inspector, what are you?" and he replies, "I AM, THAT I AM". In Exodus 3:14 when Moses asked what God's name was. God replied, "I AM THAT I AM". How can any Christian, claim the very name of the Almighty God? Manly P. Hall in his book, pages 54, 55, and 92 gives even more insight into this terrible contamination of the truth. He writes, " Man is a god in the making, and as in the mystic myths of Egypt, on the potter's wheel, he is molded. The glorious privileges of a Master Mason are in keeping with his greater knowledge and wisdom... For him the Heavens have opened, and the Great Light has bathed him in its radiance. The Prodigal Son, so long a wanderer in the regions of darkness, he has returned to his Father's house. The voice speaks from the heavens, its power thrilling the Master until his own being seems filled with its divinity, saying, 'This is my beloved son, in whom I am well pleased .' "He, the master mason, in truth has become the spokesman of the Most High! He stands between the glowing firelight and the world. Through him passes Hydra, the great snake, and from its mouth there pours to man the light of God." This is insulting to any sane man's intelligence, power of reasoning, and common sense!

Then in the 19th degree, the initiate receives the title of Grand Pontiff. After swearing an oath of secrecy and of total obedience, the "Thrice Puissant" anoints him with oil on the crown of his head and says: "Be Thou a priest forever, after the order of Melchizedek". See Scottish Rite Masonry Illustrated, The Complete Ritual, Vol 2, pages 26-27. According to the book of Hebrews 7:17, Jesus Christ is the only priest forever according to the order of Melchizedek. How blasphemous can one get? Here, I found that the Royal Priesthood power of Jesus is given to the deceiver, Lucifer, the god of Freemasonry, who hides behind mystery, ritual and allegory to snare his prey.

In the 17th degree, of Knights of the East and West, the Degree is supposed to represent the end of the world, when all good masons receive their reward by being conducted to a throne at the right hand of the ALL PUISSANT, having been purified by washing their robes in their own blood. There is a book with seven seals that only the ALL PUISSANT, (the Almighty), can open. Scottish Rite Masonry Illustrated, pages 453, 456, and 457. This is blasphemy to any Christian! What about the "Lion of the Tribe of Judah, the Root of David, JESUS, who opens the seals?" Rev. 5:5

I wish to return to the third degree, that of Master Mason, for a moment. In this degree, the candidate is raised from the dead by the master of the lodge. Here we find the lodge master taking the place of Jesus Christ , our Lord and Master, Savior and Brother. How can any Christian tolerate this to happen? And, this will not interfere with my Faith? One part of this deception is that so many millions of good Christian men have submitted to this garbage! I noticed that Lucifer has usurped the power of JESUS' Resurrection, and was now raising others from the dead! How stupid and deceiving!

In Hall's book, pages 53, 54, and 92 we find these words, "Man is a god in the making." Since Joseph Smith was a mason, is it any wonder that the Mormon Religion teaches that man can reach godhood here on Earth? Strange, that now the Mormon Church in some circles, is no longer considered to be Christian, but is a cult. Deception takes many forms and causes havoc in sundry places.

In my search, I found one other terribly blasphemous practice. In Pike's book: <u>Morals and Dogma</u> page 539, Pike writes this question; "What is to us the chief symbol of man's ultimate redemption and regeneration?" ANSWER: "The fraternal supper of bread which nourishes, and of wine which refreshes and exhilarates, symbolic of the time which is to come, when all mankind shall be one great harmonious brotherhood; and teaching these great lessons; that as matter changes ever, but no single atom is anniliated, is it not rational to suppose that the far nobler soul does not continue to exist beyond the grave; that many thousands who have died might claim to be joint owners with ourselves of the particles that compose our physical bodies; for matter ever forms new combinations' and the bodies of the ancient dead, the patriarchs before and since the flood, the kings and the common people of all ages, resolved into their constituent elements, are carried upon the wind over all continents, and continually enter into the form part of the new souls, creating new bonds of sympathy and brotherhood between each man that lives and all his race. And thus, in the bread we eat, and in the wine we drink tonight may enter into and form part of us, the identical particles of the matter that once formed parts of the material bodies called MOSES, CONFUCIUS, PLATO, SOCRATES, or JESUS OF NAZARETH. In the truest sense, WE EAT AND DRINK THE BODIES OF THE DEAD: AND CANNOT SAY THAT THERE IS A SINGLE ATOM OF OUR BLOOD OR BODY, THE OWNER-SHIP OF WHICH SOME OTHER SOUL MIGHT NOT DISPUTE WITH US."

This service is usually performed on Maundy Thursday and is a blasphemous example of desecrating the LORD'S SUPPER or HOLY COMMUNION. This is an example of the Gnostic teachings that originated in Egypt, and it is considered heretical at best. Even though I found many other examples of Lucifer's ingeniousness, I believe I have listed enough for any Christian man to realize into what he has gotten himself. This was more than enough for me. I made up my mind to get out of this organization as fast as I could. I would not only leave masonry, I would renounce if for what it really is.

Never again will I be found in a Masonic lodge of any kind, or pay dues to any of masonry's lodges. Never again will I wear the Masonic jewelry, never again will I speak its secret words, use its symbols and signs, its lingo, its organization or materials except in RENOUNCEMENT!

CHAPTER EIGHT
RENOUNCEMENT

After reaching my decision to leave and to renounce freemasonry, I went to my home, I lived alone, and at about 9:30 p.m. I began to gather all of my Masonic paraphernalia together for disposal. I went out into my back yard that was lighted by a floodlight, and had a seven-foot picket fence around it. I took a small barbecue grille and set it up. I brought my lambskin apron, my Scottish Rite cornet, my fez, my certificates, books, jewelry and anything else that I could find and lay my hands on that was Masonic. I will say that my Masonic Bible had disappeared. May heaven help whoever has it. I took all of the certificates and pages from the books and put them in the grille. It was so quiet that I heard not only the crickets, but everything else that moved. There was no wind, and the sky was clear. It was very dry in the back yard, for it was in the Wintertime, and the grass had gone into hibernation. I put the jewelry on top of the paper along with the lambskin apron and struck a match. All of a sudden, there appeared to be quite a breeze blowing. Strange- - There had been no breeze when I went out into the yard! I had only been there a few minutes. I kept striking matches until I had struck about six or seven, for I was determined to burn the material. I shouted to the darkness, "Blow on- I will burn this whether you like it or not."

In biblical days, anything that was mystical or sorcery, witchcraft, or the like was burned. After the fire started burning well, I put the fez and the cornet on the blaze. The fire and the blaze became blue and very hot. The grille was center mounted and the heat was so intense that the grille began to droop around the center post. It was ruined, but that was ok with me. The wind was blowing so hard now that the fire was getting out of the grille and onto the dry grass. This kept me busy for some time as I ran all over the yard stamping out the small blazes. I said again to the darkness, "Blow-on, I will continue until I am finished." I remembered that one of the names for Satan is 'Prince of the power of the air'. I also remember reading in the Gospels how Jesus commanded the elements to 'BE STILL'. When I had finished burning everything that I could find, pertaining to Masonry, I then took a hose and doused the fire, soaking it completely. I took a long-handled spoon and dipped the ashes out into a large paper bag, and then threw it all into the garbage can where it belonged. As I went back into the house to turn off the floodlight, I noticed that there was no breeze at all. The hair on the back of my neck and arms stood up, and I said to no one in particular, "Yes, I know beyond any shadow of a doubt, that the supernatural forces of darkness are real".

After receiving the Baptism in the Spirit, I believed that I had gone into a wilderness experience to be tempted in many ways. Please do not judge me in saying that, for I would never attempt to place myself in a like situation to what our Lord experienced. It seems that if we can hear the voice of God the Holy Spirit, then we can also hear other voices of a spiritual nature as well. I was a babe in a war, a spiritual war, and did not know which end of the rifle to put to my shoulder, because I couldn't find the rifle. I foolishly beat the air with my hands, but could not fight what I could not see. I used to question GOD, and say "Why, Father?" "Why should I have to go through this?"

One day, as I was driving home from work, I said, "Lord, please show me what this is, and why I am experiencing these things. I know there is a time and reason for everything. But don't show me with my eyes, for I am terrified now. Just show me in your word. That was on a Thursday evening- I shall never forget that. On the next Sunday afternoon, I was sitting in my den watching a football game on television, and I noticed my Bible lying on the coffee table. Something or someone urged me to pick it up. I picked it up and let it fall open wherever it liked. It came open to I Peter, chapter one and verse six. I began to read, "In this you greatly rejoice, though now for a little while, if need be, you have been grieved by various trials, that the genuineness of your faith being much more precious than gold that perishes, though it is tested by fire, may be found to praise, honor, and glory at the revelation of Jesus Christ, whom having not seen, you love." The Holy Spirit said,

"There is the answer to your prayer". I hit the floor on my knees weeping- thanking Him for his goodness and mercy. As I read on, it said "Having not seen Him, you believed- what blessedness!" Jesus was right when he said to Thomas, "Blessed are you because having seen, you believe, but I say, blessed are those who believe that have not seen." John 20:26-29 I was very happy and very humbled.

Later, I found other items of Masonic memorabilia, which I promptly destroyed. One day, while rummaging through the glove box of my car, I found my Masonic ring. Somehow, I missed it when I was gathering up all the items to be destroyed. I recalled the night when I removed it from my hand, and threw it into the glove box- I did not even want it in my pocket! While having forgotten about it, I was determined to be rid of that ring.

The next day I went to work and it rained all day. As I returned home that night I stopped on a levee between Nebo and Manitou, Kentucky. There was a channel there that was swollen with floodwaters. As I approached the channel, I again determined to be rid of that ring! There was no place to park there, but I pulled off into a small dirt road. I pulled in and stopped. I stepped out of the car and went almost over my shoes in mud. "Uh-oh, I will have trouble getting out of here." It was still raining as I grasped the ring in my right hand and began to pray. I asked forgiveness again for having been deceived and involved in something that was an abomination to GOD. I asked for strength to reject it and to reject all the horrible oaths that I had taken in order to get this ring. I drew my arm back and threw it as hard as I could into the waters of that swollen channel. The instant that ring touched the water, thunder rumbled afar off and in the distance lightening flashed. I stood with rain hitting my face, weeping and thanking GOD for leading me to the real truth of what I had done. I kicked as much mud off my shoes as I could, I re-entered my car, started the engine and immediately realized that I was stuck. I said "Father, I am going to need your help." I put the car in reverse and it started to spin. I said, "Help me, Lord." I rocked the car one more time, and there was no more spinning. The car acted as if someone was pushing it back onto the highway. For some reason, I was not surprised, I merely said, "Thank You, Lord," and drove on home.

I became more convinced than ever that Freemasonry is an abomination to the Lord, because it is a deception and a worship of Lucifer (who is Satan). I saw how deceptive he is, and how he appears as an angel of light. How he appears as one thing while in reality, he is something else. It took God, The Holy Spirit, to show me. I was blind, but when HE came into me with power, the scales fell off my eyes, to paraphrase the Apostle Paul. I truly could see now. Although I had experienced horror, torment, and out-right terror, because I know of no other way to describe it, I began to see many things in the dark world of Satan.

I went to my minister at that time who wore a ring similar to mine, and took my tape on witchcraft for him to review. He only listened to part of it, none of the part about Freemasonry. I said to him "Please, listen to this, for I must tell you that I, too, was a mason, and I must show you why this ring should come off your hand. He refused to listen to the whole tape, and I left feeling defeated. He said that he was not interested. A few weeks later, I was still sitting in church when my pastor rose and began to relate a story about something that had happened to him recently. He worked underground at the coal mine where I also worked as Manager of Employee Relations. He said, "My wife had a dream one night wherein I lost my hand in the mines." This week, I was riding a piece of equipment and my hand slipped over and was caught in the moving parts of the equipment. I screamed, "Stop, Stop!" it didn't cut my hand off, but my fingers were mashed flat. My hand was released, and no bones were broken. At that time, I remembered what Jim Shouse had said to me about my ring. Though it breaks my heart to do this, off comes this ring. I was immediately on my feet, thanking God for all his goodness and mercy. No one else in the congregation knew what I meant, because it had been a private conversation between my pastor and me. To this day, I have not seen it back on his hand. He told me that he had left the lodge and never paid dues thereafter. But I had yet to do some withdrawing from the lodge.

After reading the book, <u>Should a Christian Be A Mason</u>, I sat down and wrote a letter using the pattern in the book. I put the letter into my own words and sent it to the Blue Lodge of which I was a member in Culver City, California, and to the Scottish Rite in Germany, and finally to the Shrine in Oakland, California. This covered the four lodges wherein I had held membership.

Not long thereafter, I received a letter back from a man that I had known and who had been intrustmental in Freemasonry's work in Germany. I believe that he was the head of the Scottish Rite bodies in the American/Canadian system, or at least the bodies in Europe. He proceeded to tell me how dumb I was, in a very nice way. He said that Masonry was not a religion, and thousands of Christians had found fulfillment in Masonry. He wished me well. About two months later, I found that I had not been removed from their mailing list, for I received a bulletin. In this bulletin, Albert Pike was quoted as saying that Masonry is a religion. Double talk-deception-lies. What I had been told was that all seeing eye of GOD, turned out to be the all-seeing eye of Osiris and Lucifer. One only has to go to the book of Isaiah Chapter 14, verse 12, to find out just who Lucifer is. "How you are fallen from Heaven, O Lucifer, son of the morning! How you are cut down to the ground, You who weakened the nations!"

When I learned what the organization called the Illuminati was, and that it had been infiltrated with high-ranking masons, drunk with the quest for money and power throughout the world, I then felt justified in what I had done. My letter, I feel sure, was sent on down to other lodges of which I was a member, for I stopped getting their bulletins etc. I did receive some letters saying that I was two years behind with the dues, and if they didn't receive my dues soon, they were going to expel me from the lodge… THROW ME IN THE BRIAR PATCH! I renounced those bloody oaths and everything that I, both said and did, while under the deception of Freemasonry, and I strongly recommend the same for any mason who reads this book. I know that I have received forgiveness for those errors of mine, for The Holy Spirit has made that known to me. Philippians 4:13 says, " I can do all things through Christ who strengthens me."

One thing that I must point out here is that while I was going through these trials, my family was praying for me to see the true light about freemasonry, and that I would get out of it. The effects of prayer are amazing to say the least! It was prayer that started me on this journey. Freemasonry is so deceptive, that I would readily say that 95% of its members have no idea of what they are doing, whom they are serving, and to whom they are paying homage. All one has to do is look at the symbols of masonry. It deals heavily with symbolism.

Many of the symbols are put forward in meaning one thing, when in truth, they mean something else. In the First Degree of Entered Apprentice, the initiate is shown a point within a circle bounded by two vertical parallel lines. He is told that the point within the circle is himself and the circle is the limits of his activities in this life here on earth. The two parallel lines are said to represent John the Baptist and John the Apostle. In truth this has nothing to do with the initiate, or the two Johns. It is a phallic symbol and has been used for many years as pagans worshiped and mixed in sex with their worship.

Remember the temple prostitutes of Diana, Isis, Vishnu, and Ishtar. This garbage has been around since Nimrod and The Tower of Babel! It's time we awakened from out sleep and took note! This type of thing happened within the Feast of Tishri, and involved fertility rites. The order of the Eastern Star is an inverted pentagram with the two points of the star pointing upward, which only a few know this to be signified, as the Goat of Mendes, the devil. The square and compass is put ahead of the great light of all humanity, the Bible, the word of truth.

Chapter Nine
The Obvious Deception

The one deception that we, ordinary men, should immediately recognize is the Masonic claim that, 'Freemasonry takes good men and makes them better!' This is ridiculous, and should be immediately questioned! Just how is this accomplished? Yet, neither did I, nor any other man that I know ask, "How is this done?" We just blindly accepted it, and went on with the program. Our LORD said in Matthew 23:15 "Woe to you, Scribes and Pharisees, hypocrites! For you travel land and sea to win one proselyte, and when he is one, you make him twice as much a son of hell as yourselves." This sounds very much like a parallel passage of scripture with application to modern methods.

People seldom realize that Jesus warned more about the torment of hell, than HE spoke about the joys of Heaven.

Since hell is real, or else our Savoir was wrong, and torment lasts for all eternity, it would seem wise if we learned about our enemy and his helpers or demons. Every military leader has his way of gaining intelligence or knowledge about his enemy. This is absolutely vital to success in warfare; even Moses and Joshua sent spies into Canaan to spy out the land; where the fortifications were, weak and unprotected sites, vulnerabilities, weapons available, etc. Our enemy is extremely devious, sly and clever. Deception is the name of his game, and he is the father of lies. Since a Christian claims to follow the Lord Jesus Christ, he automatically becomes an enemy of Satan, who is bent on destruction of all mankind whether Christian or not. We are all God's creation, are HIS handiwork, and those whom HE loves very, very much. However, Satan's targets are Christians, for he already has the Non-Christian, and Jesus told us in John 16:33… "In the world you will have tribulation; but be of good cheer. I have overcome the world."

Women are not alone in using the characteristic of vanity. Men use it also. Earlier, I mentioned how I wore my Masonic ring with pride. That is pure and simple, vanity; somewhat similar to ministers who add "Doctor" to their name because of having received a PhD or doctorate in some area. Sometimes these are honorary degrees conferred by some Seminary or Bible College. This, too, is vanity, pure and simple! Does that make any one more of a Christian than the least educated ones among us? Jesus said in Matthew 23:8, "But you, do not be called Rabbi; for one is your teacher, the Christ, and you are all brothers."

As indicated earlier, Freemasonry requires a great deal of memory work. Each of the first three degrees require returning proficiency, and relating from memory what occurred In those particular degrees. How very different this world would be if the same amount of effort was spent in the study of GOD'S word! If a man can memorize this garbage, he most certainly can memorize scripture. King David said in Psalm 119:11, "Your word I have hidden in my heart, that I might not sin against you." Or do we really care enough to want to please GOD and not sin against HIM? "Vanity of vanities, All is Vanity', said Solomon. "For what profit is it to a man, if he gains the whole world, and is himself destroyed or lost?" said Jesus in Luke 9:25

We are told, empathically, in 2 Timothy 2:15 to, "Study to show yourself approved unto GOD, a workman that needs not to be ashamed, rightly dividing the word of truth." Not only does GOD'S word assist us in living the type of life that HE requires, but it also will be our judge when we stand before Christ. John 12:48, Jesus said, "HE who rejects me, and does not receive my words, has that which judges him—the word that I have spoken will judge him in the last day."

Lets not deceive ourselves with rationalization, fallacious reasoning, and lack of interest in Bible study. That book will judge us in the last day. Let's not play at Christianity or at church. Let's not waste time, energy and money at 'Lodge' work. The Masonic lodge is the greatest deception that I have encountered in my lifetime, bar none.

Chapter Ten
The Truth, Is The Truth, Is The Truth

Education can be an unnerving experience at times. Some us of learn certain lessons in a difficult fashion. The difficulty can be brought about by many factors. Some one has wisely stated, "Experience is the best teacher!" someone else added, "Because, experience is the most expensive teacher!" Trial and error is usually resorted to when we disregard or disagree with other opinions or directions. It is not always considered the best method of learning. Regardless of the reasons or methods, which we adopt and follow, many times we realize that something is amiss, and this project is not proceeding in a manner, for which we hoped.

Following the great change in my life, as mentioned earlier, I felt the need to make restitution and correct some things in my past life. The home in which I was reared was a happy, contented one; in which all members were taught responsibility, honesty, character and diligent labor. When I was first told by my spouse, the mother of my four children, that she desired a divorce from me, my world of contentment began to immediately crumble! Needless to say, the divorce came about, my family was split and my children were severely damaged, as was I.

Now, I decided that the thing I really wanted to correct was the breach in my family. I began to think that maybe reunion within the family might be a possibility. When I finally got around to mentioning this to my friends, I was amazed at the negative comments and attempts at discouraging me. This was a surprise, for I had expected encouraging remarks and advice. Some even quoted scripture to me in an effort to stop my efforts at reconciliation with my family. One friend turned to Deuteronomy 24:1-4 and read, "When a man takes a wife and marries her, and it happened that she finds no favor in his eyes because he has found some uncleanness in her, and he writes her a certificate of divorce, puts it in her hand, and sends her out of his house, when she has departed from his house, and goes and becomes another man's wife, if the latter husband detests her and writes her a certificate of divorce, puts it in her hand, and sends her out of his house, or if the latter husband dies who took her as his wife, then her <u>former husband</u> who divorced her <u>must not take her back</u> to be his wife after she has been defiled; that is an abomination before the Lord, and you shall not bring sin on the land which the LORD your GOD is giving you as an inheritance."

This did not disturb or discourage me in the least. I was ready to answer this argument. I quickly said. "That scripture does not apply to me. It was for the Jewish people who lived under the Law of Moses, and related to the land of Canaan. The Law of Moses was nailed to the cross with Jesus as found in Colossians 2:14, "Having wiped out the handwriting of requirements (Law of Moses) that was against us, which was contrary to us, and HE has taken it out of the way, having nailed it to the cross." This argument had been pounded into me for many years. The Law of Moses did not apply to Christians; otherwise, Christians would have to "Remember the Sabbath to keep it Holy." The Sabbath, the Seventh day, was a mandatory day of rest for the Jewish people. This was Saturday,, not Sunday, and Jewish people still observe the Sabbath beginning at sundown on Friday and lasting until sundown Saturday. The New Covenant, made with Israel, superseded the Old Covenant as far as living according to the Law. We, Christians are under the Perfect Law of Liberty, James 1:25. "Besides," I said, "I didn't divorce my wife, she divorced me; therefore, the scripture in Deuteronomy does not apply to me". I proceeded with my intentions, thinking all the time that this action would be pleasing to the Lord.

My ex-wife and I were re-married in Abilene, Texas, during the worship service of the church where they attended on Sunday. Our four children were present at the service, and I was very happy. After the service, my wife and I started driving to Nashville, Tennessee, where my car was parked. Before we arrived in Nashville, I think we both realized that a mistake might have been made of very serious proportions. We could hardly agree on anything! It seemed that with every two steps forward that we took, we found ourselves going one step backward.

A very hard lesson for us humans is that no matter how good our intentions may be, we can very often be wrong in our actions. If we find that we can perceive messages and guidance from GOD, THE HOLY SPIRIT, we must be wary for we probably can receive messages from other sources as well. Our impulses can cause us to err, and in this life, we are constantly in danger of being in error on a multitude of subjects. In this life, there is no guarantee against making mistakes. There is no insurance against temptation, and while many people would say to me that if I have been filled with THE HOLY SPIRIT, I should be able to handle any situation and not be guilty of sin. I am reminded that the beloved Apostle Paul who had seen Jesus, and had been filled with THE HOLY SPIRIT, was also given a "thorn in the flesh, a messenger of Satan to buffet me lest I be exalted above measure." 2 Corinthians 12:7. It would seem reasonable to me to think that if Paul was allowed to be harassed by Satan, should not the rest of us also be in the same boat?

Apparently, GOD had a lesson that HE wanted me to learn. We must be led by THE HOLY SPIRIT and not follow the desires of the flesh. In Proverbs 14:12, we find these words, "There is a way that seems right to a man, but its end is the way of death." It matters not what we think or believe; what matters is, what does GOD'S word have to say about the subject. Our opinion is worth one full gulp of muddy water!

In retrospect, I have found that I have been misled by well-meaning people who used conventional wisdom in their advice. I found that I had to unlearn some things, start

over, and realize that personal opinion and prejudices sometimes find their way into sermons and religious advice.

The great lesson that I learned in the remarriage to my
wife was that every one of the six hundred thirteen (613)
laws given to Moses by GOD, was for the benefit of the
people. GOD needs nothing; HE made us for HIMSELF
and HIS SON. Even though the old Law, the Law of Moses, did not, and does not, apply to Christians, truth is still
truth is still truth! According to Paul in 2 Timothy 3:16,17,
"All Scripture is given by inspiration of GOD, and is profit-
able for doctrine, for reproof, for correction, for instruction
in righteousness, that the man of GOD may be complete,
thoroughly equipped for every good work." If we do not
avail ourselves of Old Testament Scriptures, and the truth
therein; we discard 75% of GOD'S word!

The lesson that I very sorely learned is, 'Don't try to im-
prove on GOD'S word, and don't try to twist it to our own
selfish usage! Need I say that this remarriage didn't last? It
appeared that we were both miserable 90% of the time, finally gave up, and ended this obvious mistake in judgment.
It became apparent that infallibility was certainly not a part
of my personality, and even when trying to change a situation for the better, we still can be wrong and are subject to
many mistakes. We can and often do, deceive ourselves!

Being deceived happens more often to us than we really realize, or wish to admit! It appears that the adversary,
Satan, has a field day with much of our lives. The Webster
definition of the word, deceive, includes; 'to take in, ensnare,
catch by guile, delude, dupe, hoodwink, bamboozle, outwit
and double-cross. How many ways there are to deceive us!
And from scripture, it appears as time goes on, the decep-
tions will increase. In 2 Timothy 3:13, Paul writes, "But

evil men will grow worse and worse, deceiving and being deceived." Then in Ephesians 5:6 we find, "Let no one deceive you with empty words, for because of these things the wrath of GOD comes upon the sons of disobedience." Galatians 6:7, tells us rather pointedly, "<u>Do not be deceived</u>, GOD is not mocked; for whatever a man sows, that he will also reap." We should and <u>must</u> be constantly on guard against deception in all its many forms.

Chapter Eleven
Grace

It should be obvious to the reader that my discovery of the deception inherent in Freemasonry did not occur as a result of displeasure with the 'Lodge' or friction with another person. GOD, THE HOLY SPIRIT led me in making the discovery, finding the books, and written materials concerning Freemasonry, and finally arriving at the realization of what I had done. As we advance in age, and begin to look back in retrospect, it is then that we recognize that GOD has had his hand on us for many years, and in ways unrecognizable at the time of occurrence. The age of GRACE is as real as rain! The following account will testify to the wonderful Grace that GOD has poured out on me during my lifetime, and I would be remiss if I didn't give HIM praise and glory for his goodness.

When I was five years old, and being the last addition to a large family, I found myself with chores for which I was ill prepared. For instance, I was baby-sitting two of my young nieces on a pallet under a large oak tree while their parents were busy in a near by field. Suddenly, a cow decided that I must have looked like a dog or some other animal, and promptly began trying to gore me. She had me on the ground and giving me a good rolling when my sister-in-law came up with a hoe and ran the cow off. There was no stock law where I lived at the time.

Then a year later, at a Thanksgiving Program in school, my brother ran over me with our car. I still remember the hot oil dripping in my face as they pulled me out from underneath the car. Fortunately for me, I had no broken bones and no internal injuries, just bruises, scrapes and contusions.

By the age of nine, I was helping my older brother load an old truck without a cab, with firewood for our home. It was very hot, and we had no water with us. We finished loading and jumped upon the seat. My brother released the brake and tried to start the engine by putting the truck in gear while going likety-split down through the woods. He couldn't get the truck in gear, and yelled to me to 'Jump'! I stood up to jump and the truck hit a tree, throwing me off, and the wood on top of me. I had bruises and lacerations all over, but no broken bones. WOW!

At age ten, even though I had lived in the country to that point, and was familiar with the outdoors and at home in the forests, I still had not learned to swim. One Saturday, my brother, my sister, and I, with several others, went swimming in a lake. In a nutshell, the sloping bottom of the lake introduced me, rather quickly, to water that was over my head. As I began to flounder about and struggle, I suddenly felt something touch me. It was my sister, who also couldn't swim. I grabbed her and pulled her under the water. I remember opening my eyes, saw little bubbles around me in the water, discovered that it was not painful to breath in water and promptly came to the conclusion that I was going to die! Then I became unconscious. When I regained consciousness, I found myself lying on the ground, gasping for air and coughing a lot. My brother had rescued me, while a lifeguard got my sister out. How ironic! The next day I was baptized along with my sister in another lake. The church that we attended had no baptistery, and a lake was used. Next year I learned to swim!

At the ripened age of sixteen, while traveling to a high school basketball game, the pickup truck, in which I was riding with four other teenagers, flipped over and rolled into a deep ditch. None of us were seriously injured. I received a large lump on my forehead, but was able to continue on to the game. In fact, I played in that game, and it was one of my better performances!

Next year, while swimming in a creek, i.e., 'the ole swimin' hole' for us young country guys, my foot slipped as I dived from a thirty-foot high bank into the water. Realizing that I was about to hit shallow water, I rolled up into a ball while turning my head off to one side. I did hit the creek bottom on my left shoulder, fracturing my left collarbone. Had I not turned my head, for whatever reason, I will never know, my neck, most surely, would have been broken.

During my military career, I was assigned a position as Detachment Commander of a unit at Point Barrow, Alaska. During that year, in the Land of the Mid-night Sun, I was caught in two different "white-outs". This is a condition wherein the ground, the sky, and the air all appear to be white. A person has no depth perception, and should he leave his vehicle, he would likely become dinner for the nearest polar bear. There was only one thing to do in a situation such as this, and that was to remain in one's vehicle all day or all night until rescue people arrived in a tracked vehicle. I spent two long nights in my vehicle, in this manner.

While stationed at Point Barrow, I encountered another hazard that had never entered my mind. While visiting the one Doctor and one Dentist in the village of Barrow, one of the largest Eskimo Settlements in Alaska, and being on my way back to the camp in which I lived, I stopped by an Eskimo's house to pick up a friend who lived in the same camp as I. As I left my engine running and approached the front of the house, I noticed something white moving in the unlit snow-break. It was a drunken Eskimo in a tee shirt who was trying to force his way into the house where a party was in progress. The people inside the house did not want him to come in, so they were holding the door. The Eskimo asked me who I was, and pushed me outside the small room. I was dressed in a Parka with the hood up, heavy pants, mukluk boots and mittens as the temperature was 20 degrees below zero. I didn't want any trouble, so I backed outside.

Then the man ran by me into the house next door, and I quickly stepped back into the snow-break, hammered on the door, identified myself, and called to my friend that if he wanted a ride back to camp, he must come out now! The next thing that I knew, the Eskimo had returned with a two-foot long skinning knife with which he planned to use to pry the door open. He said to me, "I told you to leave," and he started jabbing me in the stomach with his long knife. I quickly backed out of the building, I had absolutely nothing with which to defend myself, and tried to back away from him. From out of nowhere, two other Eskimo men ran up, grabbed the man with the knife, and told me to go, now! Into my vehicle I went, and left with out my friend!

While flying from Japan to the Island of Guam once, I noticed that we were constantly in bad weather at about 15,000 feet altitude. Unknown to us, and not forecast to happen, a Typhoon was forming, and we went right through the middle of it. Many of our passengers experienced airsickness, but we were much too busy to notice. With an old airplane and poor equipment, this can be a formable task, to say the least!

Once, over the North Atlantic Ocean, at night and in rough weather conditions, while in route from Scotland to the United States, an engine failed and began to backfire loudly. This caused great concern among our passengers, to say nothing of the crewmembers. I diverted the aircraft to the airport nearest to our position. The weather was bad there, but we could not continue against strong head winds to the U.S., and there was insuffcient fuel to return to Scotland or Ireland. Our options were narrowed to one place, Iceland. The weather there had a 200-foot ceiling of clouds and one-half mile visibility with cross winds on the runway and moderate rain. At 200 feet altitude, the runway and approach lights were not visible. I descended 50 more feet, which was below my minimum altitude, and the runway was sighted. We landed after fighting the crosswind and rain. I was shaking so hard afterward that I could not sign the aircraft form. But as I left the flight deck, the passengers were still on board and they began to applaud. I think they were just as thankful, as was I, to be alive and to be safely on the ground.

Again on another flight from Dallas to Sacramento, California, at night and in weather, two engines, both on the same side of the aircraft failed. I made an emergency landing in Cedar City, Utah. This airport had no control tower and only the most basic of approach devices. Since we could not maintain altitude over the mountains, I was determined to get the plane on the ground as soon as possible. The landing was uneventful and no one was hurt.

Flying for many years, one finds many things that can, and do, occur that may create a bit of concern for one's safety and longevity! I have encountered thunderstorms when they were not expected over Italy, the Pyranees Mountains between France and Spain, and in a small corridor that we were required to remain in, while flying to and from, Berlin, Germany. We usually had very important persons on board, for instance, the President or the Chancellor of West Germany, and we were always shadowed by East German and Russian fighter aircraft.

In 1961, while living in Southern, California, I was involved in an auto accident wherein I suffered a broken neck, broken thumb, cracked ribs and numerous bruises and lacerations. Then, in 1980 near Wheatcroft, Kentucky, another accident produced a broken back and other injuries as well.

While flying the company plane in 1981, I found myself upside down over the Sturgis, Kentucky, airport at 500 feet altitude under the effects of a thunderstorm. Yet the landing was safe with no injuries or damage to the aircraft.

In 1991, while mowing my yard, which is steep in places, with my riding lawnmower, the mower flipped over backwards on top of me, fracturing my left shoulder. I have known of others who didn't walk away from this sort of thing!

Finally, in 1994, following a Cursillo Retreat weekend, I suffered a Heart Attack. It seemed that whenever I tried to do some work for the LORD; I noticed resistance directed toward me. Why then, have I listed all these close shaves and times when I looked death in the face? Because, these are irrefutable proof to me of GOD'S grace, mercy and protection. One reason that I am still alive, I believe, is so that this great deception, which I have listed, may be known to honest, unsuspecting Christian men who have suffered the same deception as I.

In this age of GRACE, the last stage before the return of our LORD JESUS CHRIST, it would be wise if the men who read this would begin to seriously investigate the untruthful claims of Freemasonry. Vanity is not worth the expectation of something that most definitely will not occur. If the HOLY BIBLE is true, and I assuredly believe that it is, then there in only one way to the Father, King of the Universe, and that is through HIS son, JESUS THE CHRIST. It would seem reasonable to me that I look for Heaven, and not the myth of that great lodge in the sky.

Chapter Twelve
Summation And Final Word

I cannot, in all good conscience, ask the question, why do all men allow themselves to be deceived by these things, because I did the very same thing. Without a family that cared about me and prayed for me, I would probably have gone on feeling that everything was fine. Even after I had cleared my house of all Masonic memorabilia, I still had occasions of harassment by a spirit. One of the gifts, of God the Holy Spirit, is the 'discerning of spirits'. I Corinthians 12:10. I believe at the time of my harassment, I had that gift and at times, I still do. It is not a gift for the faint-hearted that is for sure! I do not believe that the power that came against me was some minor demon; I believe it was much more powerful than that, Ephesians 6:12 says, " For we do not wrestle against flesh and blood, but against principalities, against powers, against the rulers of the darkness of this age, against spiritual hosts of wickedness in the heavenly places." The world of the spiritual is very real, even though it is unseen, while the physical world is but a copy that will pass away at the right time.

I asked GOD over and over why it was necessary for me to go through this trial. One day, after asking the same question over again, the answer came so quickly that it shocked me. The answer was, "Because you were in the occult". Having gone through my ordeal, I finally realized that Masonry is indeed occultic. Even the Masonic writers, themselves, testify to this fact. The occultic forces with whom I had been following, apparently did not want to turn me loose. But Jesus defeated Satan and made him a laughing stock while stripping him of his power and authority. Satan is a liar and the father of lies. He comes to steal, kill, and destroy, John 10:10.

The gifts of, GOD, the Holy Spirit, are given severally, as He wills and as He wishes. I do not know all the answers- I have wondered many times why these things happened, I kept talking to the Lord and asking Him, "Lord, what am I to do with this knowledge?" A man once came to our congregation who had the gift of the word of knowledge- prophecy, if you will. He once said to me that all those bad things that you did in your past life will now be used for good in order to help someone who is undergoing similar circumstances. They will be used for the glory of GOD and Him, only.

Are our prayers merely monologues? Do we ever take time to listen for an answer? One way that our prayers are answered is when we put our minds in neutral and completely relax, a thought will come winging in and our first reaction is "where did that come from, I wasn't thinking about that subject." It gets our attention. We should practice spending time alone with GOD and let our prayers become more than just a one-way conversation. One- way is no conversation at all! I have always 'prided myself' in being a logical thinker, with my emotions completely under control. But when the supernatural became real to me, I was in a quandary as to how to deal with it. I believe that this narrative confirms that. Yet, a scripture kept coming to my mind that is found in 2 Timothy 1:7, "For GOD has not given us a spirit of fear, but of power and of love and of a sound mind." This was a great comfort to me during my time of trial.

I am convinced that the powers that I dealt with during this time were not from GOD, but from the powers of darkness. Of course, they can do nothing without GOD'S approval or allowance. Part of the confusion that I felt was due to fear. If you search the Bible, you will find that anytime a spiritual being came into contact with a human, the human experienced great fear. He usually became prostrate with fear as in the case of Daniel, the soldiers who guarded the tomb of Jesus, and the Apostle John on the Isle of Patmos when he saw Christ in his glorified state. So, I do not pretend to sit in judgment as to what happened, but I do know this: It stirred me into action on two fronts. The first direction was to turn to GOD, and seek Him with all my being. I went seeking, asking, and knocking. The scriptures are correct in every detail. I received, I found, and the door came open to me. The other direction, was turning away from Freemasonry, and not only quitting going to the lodge and paying dues, I renounced it for what it is, the greatest deception of my life. My life is now devoted to the service of GOD and the furtherance of the Gospel of Jesus Christ and His church. Although I had been a church member for thirty-five years before this happened, I am convinced that I am now closer to The Lord than ever before.

Oh, yes, the enemy still comes against me to tempt, harass, and torment. But I think that I have now learned how to deal with him, without always being on the short end of the stick. I always remember that Peter said in I Peter 5:8, "Be sober, be vigilant; because your adversary, the devil, walks about like a roaring lion, seeking whom he may devour."

You men who read this and find that you, too, may have been deceived by masonry, I say this, "Get out of it as fast as you can." I'm not asking you to take my word for it, investigate for yourselves! Read the writings of the Bigwigs, the authors of Masonic books who describe the 'craft' for themselves. Find out what masonry really stands for- who serves it, and why the name Jesus Christ is never allowed in the prayers of the lodge chaplain. And this doesn't interfere with your Christianity? Can you really get to heaven through good graces of the great lodge in the sky? Jesus said in John 10:1,2 and 7, "Most assuredly, I say to you, he who does not enter the sheepfold by the door, but climbs up some other way, the same is a thief and a robber. But he who enters by the door is the shepherd of the sheep." Then Jesus said to them again, "Most assuredly, I say to you, I am the door of the sheep." Find out for yourself, for one day we will all stand before god and give an account for the things done in the body. I sincerely hope that you are not one of those people who confess to being a Christian and member of some body that you don't even know for what it stands.

One other thing; do not fear the persecution of Satan or the members of the lodge. They will not fulfill those bloody oaths that you swore on the Bible. Anyone who commits murder will be prosecuted, and even masons know that! Get on your knees and pray to GOD for forgiveness, and that you may have time yet to renounce masonry in all its forms and facets- whether it be the Blue Lodge, the Knights Templar, the Scottish Rite, the Shrine, the Eastern Star, Demolay, Rainbow Girls or Job's Daughters. You can prove the deception for yourself, if you will only investigate. Do not fear the loss of prestige. What is prestige but vanity? "Ah, vanity of vanities- all is vanity," said Solomon. Do not fear the loss of your job- fear only God Almighty. Do not be a deceived servant of the devil. Get out of it, and call it like you see it- a deception. I am so grateful that the HOLY SPIRIT showed the deception to me. I know the revelation was most certainly not by Lucifer or his minions from hell. I know that I would never have stumbled upon the answers that I found all by myself. Again, the secrecy of masonry is absolutely silly. Keep in mind that there are no secrets from GOD! We cannot hide anything from HIM. HIS word tells us in 2 Corinthians 6:14. "Do not be unequally yoked together with unbelievers, for what fellowship has light with darkness and CHRIST with Belial?"

You may say, "Well, I know that I am not deceived." One never knows when he is being deceived. If that were not true, there would be no deception; Eve didn't know she was being deceived in the Garden of Eden. If you are aware of the deception, and still don't care about it, then you are like Adam. He was not deceived. He committed treason against the MOST HIGH GOD. GOD has a name and it is not "The Great Architect of the Universe". That name is found nowhere in the Bible; it is a manufactured name just like all the other things in Freemasonry from paganism! OUR FATHER is indeed, the creator of the Universe, but HE is so very much more than that. If you really examine the writings of masonry, the teachings of the fraternity, and remain therein, then you've either hardened your heart or just plain will not see. "None is so blind as him who will not see!" GOD told Ezekiel, "Son of man, go and speak to the children of Israel. If you do not, I will require their blood of you, but if you go and speak my word, and they do not hearken to it, their blood will be on their own heads." Brothers, since you have been told, what you do now will determine whether or not your blood is put on your own head. IN JESUS' NAME, AMEN.

ABOUT THE AUTHOR

Jim Shouse was born in Prentiss County, Mississippi, the youngest of eleven children. His parents, highly regarded throughout the area in which he grew up, were strong, devout Christians. His younger years were spent in rural America; he attended High School in Wheeler, Mississippi, and Community College in Booneville, Mississippi. He is a graduate of the University of Nebraska at Omaha, and did Graduate work at Southern Illinois University, Edwardsville, Illinois.

He served twenty-two years as Pilot, Navigator and Observer in the United States AirForce, retiring as a Lieutenant Colonel. His last assignment, accomplished in West Germany during the Cold War, was especially fulfilling. As Aircraft Commander of USAF multi-engine aircraft, his passengers included;the President of West Germany, Gustav Heinemann and his governmental team, the Chancellor of West Germany, Willie Brandt, the CommanderOf the United States Air Forces Europe and later Chairman of the Joint Chiefs of Staff, David Jones, the Commander of the Strategic Air Command, General Dougherty, and numerous Senators, Congressmen, and other very important Persons.

He is the father of one son and three daughters, and makes his home in Morganfield, Kentucky. As a retiree from the USAF, a local business, and Spoken Word Ministries, wherein he performed six biblical characters in First Person Narrative throughout eleven different states, he now devotes himself to speaking engagements and serving our DEAR LORD.